GLAD AND SORRY SEASONS

GLAD & SORRY SEASONS

CATHERINE CHANDLER

BIBLIOASIS
Windsor, Ontario

FIRST EDITION

Library and Archives Canada Cataloguing in Publication

Chandler, Catherine, 1950-, author
        Glad and sorry seasons / written by Catherine Chandler.

Poems.
Some poems are translations from French and Spanish.
Issued in print and electronic formats.
ISBN 978-1-927428-61-0 (pbk.).--ISBN 978-1-927428-62-7 (epub)

        I. Title.

PS8605.H35615G53 2014   C811'.6   C2013-907311-6
                                                 C2013-907312-4

Biblioasis acknowledges the ongoing financial support of the Government of Canada through the Canada Council for the Arts, Canadian Heritage, the Canada Book Fund; and the Government of Ontario through the Ontario Arts Council and the Ontario Media Development Corporation.

Edited by Eric Ormsby
Copy-edited by Tara Murphy
Typeset and designed by Kate Hargreaves

PRINTED AND BOUND IN CANADA

CONTENTS

PART I: GIVE SORROW WORDS

Coming to Terms	11
Two Poems of the Sea	12
i. The Dawning	
ii. To a Minor Goddess	
The Flying Moment	13
Vinegar Tree	14
Full Snow Moon	15
The Measure of Their Days	16
The Crag	17
Intervals	18

PART II: DRIVING BACK SHADOWS

After a Line by Millay	21
A Fieldstone Fence	22
Haiku	23
The Ovenbird	24
Breva	25
Bequeathal	26
November	27
Winterbourne	28

PART III: THE OLDEST SINS

SALIGIA: Seven Deadly Sonnets

i.	Superbia	31
ii.	Acedia	32
iii.	Luxuria	33
iv.	Invidia	34
v.	Gula	35
vi.	Ira	36
vii.	Avaritia	37

PART IV: WITH MIRTH AND LAUGHTER

Sonnet Love   41
The Bard   42
All These Words   44
A Mother's Kyrielle   45
When   46
Boxing Day Prayer   47
Rush Hour Sonondilla   48
She   49
In Retrospect   50

PART V: A SMACK OF ALL NEIGHBOURING LANGUAGES

Five French Canadian (Québec) Poets

Léon-Pamphile Le May: My Childhood Home   53
Louis-Honoré Fréchette: Niagara   54
Louis Dantin: The Stars   55
Albert Lozeau: It's Raining   56
Émile Nelligan: The Passerby   57

Five Spanish American (Southern Cone) Women Poets

María Eugenia Vaz Ferreira: The Mysterious Star 58
Delmira Agustini: The Wonderful Boat   59
Gabriela Mistral: The Sonnets of Death (I)   60
Alfonsina Storni: Inheritance   61
Juana de Ibarbourou: Rebel   62

PART VI: GLAD AND SORRY SEASONS

The Lost Villages: Inundation Day   65
Upheavals   67
Heartwood   68
The Red Beads   69
Ragbag   70
Beach Dogs   71
Críonnacht   72
Waiting   74
Edward Hopper's *Automat*   75

Notes   77

In memory of my father
Ex tenebris ad lumen

PART I
GIVE
SORROW
WORDS

COMING TO TERMS

I set aside my white smocked cotton blouse,
my pants with the elastic belly panel.
The only music in the empty house
strains from a distant country western channel.
My breasts are weeping. I've been given leave—
a week in which to heal and convalesce.
I peel away the ceiling stars; unweave
the year I'd entered on your christening dress.

I rearrange my premises—perverse
assumptions!—gather unripe figs; throw out
the bloodied bedclothes; scour the universe
in search of you. And God. And go about
my business as my crooked smile displays
the artful look of ordinary days.

TWO POEMS OF THE SEA

i. The Dawning

The sea, relentless in her give-and-take,
her rising, falling waves that seem to make
amends in silence just before they break
ashore, reflects the instant I awake—

a moment of reprieve, when every snake
I realize is fantasy or fake;
when life's a bowl of cherries. Piece of cake.
(There must have been some terrible mistake…)

And then the crash. The undertow. The ache.

ii. To a Minor Goddess

Wave on wave all heaving and arch and spillage;
blue and green and grey overlaid with silver.
Christmas Day—my saviour the South Atlantic.
          Triumph. Surrender.

All my gods have failed me, yet Achelois,
you have watched me wavering in the billows;
you have heard me weeping the wail of seagulls,
          and you have answered:

Do not look for eyes in the dancing diamonds;
do not long for lullabies in the breakers;
do not lend more tears to the salt of oceans'
          flotsam and jetsam.

Listen for the crash. See the string of seafoam
lace that hems the sand with a hush and whisper.
Silence. Nothing. Everything. Constellations.
          Guardian angels.

THE FLYING MOMENT

One season, back in '65,
when cups and saucers came alive,

when time stood down—and up—to death,
when dark dimensions, length and breadth,

soared off with senses, bees and birds
in a futility of words,

a purple, orange, silver kiss
anointed ignorance with bliss.

But now the world's a shadow box
of butterflies. And there are clocks:

the sun comes up, the moon goes down.
Love's just another common noun.

Yet—somewhere—constellations swirl
above a fifteen-year-old girl.

VINEGAR TREE

Late Fall. The staghorn sumac's crown
is now ablaze. Though geese have flown,
the tree's red conic drupes will feed
the phoebes, thrush and grouse in need
of food through months of ice and snow.
But brew the bitter tufts just so,
and they can etch a pearl. I know.
For I have gathered up its seed,
fair-weather love, and drunk it down.

FULL SNOW MOON

The moon is full again. A latticed frost
clings to my window, while the crystal crust
of Lake Saint Louis glows as if embossed
with pearls this February night. It must
be twenty-five below. I search for words
of warmth the Guaraní alone must know
to trace their land of butterflies and birds
I made my own a mere four weeks ago.

She waxes and she wanes; she's counted on,
through human inconsistency and pride,
to reverence the rising sun each dawn
and keep her promise to the ocean tide.
But Luna's is a distant, lurid face,
her silent *O* no answer as to how
on earth I'll ever find the grit and grace
to muddle through to spring, one moon from now.

THE MEASURE OF THEIR DAYS

The wringer washer churned in perfect time
in back-and-forth slish-sloshing. With its song,
two sisters would sidestep and sing along.
Fels-Naptha flakes took care of grease and grime.
They'd hear its rhythmic cadence rise and fall
then fall and rise. This turnaround and switch
teased the girls who needed to know which
approach was true. Their mother said it all
would come out in the wash. Yet to this day
the mystery is unsolved. At any rate,
the agitator seemed to calibrate
the heart of matters. As it plugged away
between two wars their world shone clean and bright.
Years later, they would march.
Left.
Right.

THE CRAG

From the end of the earth will I call unto thee,
when my heart is overwhelmed: Lead me to the rock
that is higher than I. (Psalm 61:2)

The hours buckle, folding into pleats,
and meet like valley synclines, while the moon
is waning on Mom's alabaster sheets.
Days collapse in pure duration. Noon.
Then six. Saint Nicholas's church bells chime
the Angelus. A spatial instant, long
in coming, blinks in geologic time.
I hum her favorite Frank Sinatra song.

Gone is the golden mountain of our youth;
gone is its rarefied reality.
Still, there lies an element of truth
amid this crushing verticality.
Down. Down in history we go;
past anthracite, the colour of all woe.

INTERVALS

The years had stacked.
This route between two points left him perplexed:
which path was true? Thus at a loss, appalled
(he'd always liked things neat, exact:
loose pennies rolled
in tidy wrappers, weed-free gardens walled,
addresses Rolodexed,
each day appraised, accounted for, controlled),

last night he thought
he'd catalogue his cars and toys. They all
appeared: the old Suburban and of course
the brand-new Buick Skylark bought
in sixty-five,
his Comet sled, his wooden hobby horse,
but he could not recall
the Saturn Astra parked out in the drive.

He'd tabulate
the names of every person he had met
at every stage along his fourscore life—
the ones he'd loved or chanced to hate—
and he would limn
Brick Bradford in detail, but not his wife,
though he could not forget
the music box she'd purchased on a whim.

Another dawn
has slipped through window blinds to find him still
attempting to remember parables,
a nephew's face, the word *chiffon*,
the Seven Seas;
to place at last the ordered variables,
those nested n's that fill
the space between his dark parentheses.

PART II
DRIVING
BACK
SHADOWS

AFTER A LINE BY MILLAY

Grow not too high, grow not too far from home,
she asks the tree, not wishing it be sparse
or stunted; simply that it cease to raise
up heavenward; instead, to send its root,
its mother-strength, to crack the rock apart.

She asks it delve beyond what soil and rain
provide, past bones, beneath the precious ore;
descending ever deeper, to the core,
the furnace fuelling every pulsing vein—
the bottom line, the base, the hub. The heart.

The tree is bare now, yet it bore the fruit
of each notation, each uncluttered phrase;
the earthy words she dared the world to parse:
the susurrations of her whispering dome.

A FIELDSTONE FENCE

A fieldstone fence still stands today
where long ago a settler passed
his plow. Though years have given way,
a fieldstone fence still stands today
deep in the woods. Although it may
well be the living can't outlast
a fieldstone fence, I stand today
where long ago a settler passed.

HAIKU

haru:

a bush warbler sings
beside the snowmelt river
through mist-muffled air

natsu:

white shoes, handkerchiefs
first tea on the balcony
an evening rainbow

aki:

river of heaven
stars flow out across the night
gathering lanterns

fuyu:

in a withered field
she seeks forgotten flowers
dreams of camellias

THE OVENBIRD

In Uruguay, in spring, I've often heard
lighthearted trills along a dusty road:
the lively, undiminished ovenbird
sings as she builds her intricate abode.
The wily swallow, with no stringent code
of constancy, surveys the chambered nest;
and knows that, following this episode
of eggs with which the other bird is blessed,
he'll snatch the abdicated space. Hard-pressed
though he may be for time, for love, for will,
too wise to prove an uninvited guest,
he waits it out upon a windowsill.
The ovenbird, deemed artless by the swallow,
to practiced eyes is one tough act to follow.

BREVA

Define the springtime apple and the pear
      where
blossoms burst forth in the line of duty:
      Beauty.
Yet veiled behind an unadorned disguise
      lies
the fig tree's secret—simple, ancient, wise—
sweet florets grow, though hidden in the fruit,
and goodness rises from the rough grey root
where beauty lies.

BEQUEATHAL

For Caitlin and Steven

Unlike the lilac bush that knows
its spikes will weather winter's snows,
I've yet to find the wherewithal
to rightly come to terms with fall.

In forests full of empty nests,
withered boughs, November guests,
I seek but find no feathered thing,
no green remembrances of spring.

All that I have, now summer's gone,
are love notes from a lexicon.
My gift to you, this fragile bud—
inheritance of ink and blood.

NOVEMBER

November is a season all its own—
a month of saints and souls and soldiers. Snow
will soon white out a fallacy of brown.
It is a month of waiting, lying low.

November is a season all its own—
a time for turning back the clock as though
it's useless to pretend. A dressing-down.
Thin ice entices me to touch and go.

November's neither there nor there, but here
in dazzling dawns that dissipate to grey;
here in the tilting asymmetric branch
and sharp note of a towering white pine where
the pik and churlee of a purple finch
can either break a heart or make a day.

WINTERBOURNE

December at this latitude is stark,
the woods a snarl of black and brown and grey.
By five o'clock the west's already dark.
On the sandpit pond, now set along its edges,
straggling greylags land then hie away
while redpolls huddle deeper in the hedges.
Whitetail forage in the field and browse
on brittle forbs untouched by moldboard plows.

Then every year, around this time, a stream
loosens from the underlime of summer's
stranglehold. And when the morning steam
dissipates above the flinty bed
like idle gossip or unfounded rumours,
a song arising from its fountainhead
trips over still, impenetrable stones
into my house, my heart, my blood, my bones.

It babbles things which in July lie laden
with sunny dispositions; things that cry
out from lengthened shadows; things forbidden;
of many-splendoured things; of things that wilt,
weep, bleed and ultimately die.
And though the rivulet retreats to silt
come spring, it sings me all I need to know,
flanked though I be by behemoths of snow.

PART III
THE
OLDEST
SINS

SALIGIA: Seven Deadly Sonnets

SUPERBIA

The French funambulist of world renown
has come to carry out his daring act.
A swarm of tourists overruns the town;
bets are placed, escarpment benches packed.
Two hundred feet atop the misty pit,
with unaffected ease and nimble tread,
he sends the anxious crowd into a fit
of frenzy, tumbling, standing on his head.

The Great Blondin requests a volunteer
to piggyback across… a sudden hush
descends, betraying both desire and fear.
Tant pis!, he teases, perched above the rush
of raging water, waving to us all.
We hold our breath… and wait for him to fall.

(Niagara Falls, 1859)

ACEDIA

You've seen him at the gym, the puffed-up puppy
on the treadmill, going nowhere fast;
the Volvo-driving, Twitter-texting yuppie,
the DINK, the wine and cheese enthusiast.
A trainer and a personal assistant
plan his every move from A to Z.
Blasé, his urbane life is child-resistant;
designer drugs dispel his deep ennui.

But nights are something else. The masquerades
have tired him out. He mouths a lame excuse
for love; and when Orion dips and fades
he asks the morning silence, *What's the use?*
She finds him, later, hanging in the stair-
well. He didn't care he didn't care.

LUXURIA

The grown-ups called her Boots. Stilettoed. Brash.
Hayna Valley girl. All skin-on-bone.
Afternoons, impassive as a stone,
she'd strut downtown to trade her time for cash
from randy college boys. As rumours flew, it
made me perk my ears. Living next door,
I learned new words like *incest, jailbait, whore*.
As for her real name, I never knew it.

And then she moved. The Amy Vanderbilts
sang hallelujahs. Thanked their lucky stars.
Boots could not belong. She came from Mars,
thumbing her nose at coffee klatches, quilts,
silk stockings, and the picket fences of
Earth's fond contrivances passed off as love.

INVIDIA

A scant handful of people stand beside
his grave, and I am one of them. His wife
ignores me. When I heard that he had died
I secretly rejoiced. His was a life
of pure divertimento; mine a bane,
a counterpoint of reverence and grudge.
His popularity, no doubt, shall wane;
posterity will be the final judge.

The man is dead, but I am here to mourn
his music, held to rapturous acclaim;
and though I curse the day that he was born,
I bless the vagaries of fate and fame.
A most horrific, premature decease—
Mozart is dead. And may he rot in peace.

GULA

She stood behind me in the checkout queue
last Saturday. She mentally weighed in
on items in my shopping cart. I knew
her thoughts: *It's no small wonder she's not thin
like me. Look at that junk food—cookies, chips,
that pint of Häagen-Dazs, those salted nuts…*
She sized me up and down from head to hips
and measured both our budgets and our butts.

Clairvoyant she was not. Had she but seen
as with the scanner's unassuming eye,
she might have figured out a lifetime lean
and hard. Before I wheeled my week's supply
of relish out into the parking lot,
I whispered, *Lady, this is all I've got.*

IRA

The cheeky CEO—half-drunk, irate,
more sauce denied him—staggered to first class,
slapped down a flight attendant, bared his ass
and defecated on a dinner plate.
And then there was that weird kid down the block
who went to school hell-bent on a vendetta,
packed bitter rage alongside a Beretta,
an HP9 Norinco and a Glock.

Not quite the brutal killer nor the creep,
in quiet desperation, some of us
might temper fury with a finger, cuss
or try tai chi; while others opt to keep—
in case they ever need it, close, discreet—
a baseball bat beneath the driver's seat.

AVARITIA

They say Imelda owned three thousand pair
of shoes. The ones with Duracells would flash
as she merengued on the dance floor. She
would buy, with tidy sums of laundered cash,
Gucci platforms, pumps from Givenchy,
Ferragamo flip-flop leisurewear;
not to mention Halston golden calf-
skin spike-heeled boots. Her size, eight-and-a-half.

She ran the Beatles out of town, pell-mell,
then fled herself, accused of gross misdeeds.
Back in Manila now, she struts, undaunted,
in cap-toe slingback sandals by Chanel.
Lennon was right. Love's all one really needs.
Perhaps that's all Imelda's ever wanted.

PART IV
WITH
MIRTH &
LAUGHTER

SONNET LOVE

I love the way its rhythm and its rhymes
provide us with a promise, a belief
familiar voices at specific times
may modulate unmanageable grief.

I love the way we're called to referee
the mind-heart match-up in its scanty ring;
how through it all our only guarantee
is that for fourteen rounds the ropes will sing.

I love the way it makes us feel at home,
the way it welcomes fugitives and fools
who have forgotten all roads lead to Rome
from shared beginnings in the tidal pools.

Life's unpredictability defies
clean dénouement. I love the way it tries.

THE BARD

Our hands are full of business: let's away,
and on our actions set the name of right;
with full bags of spices, a passport, too,
for we must measure twenty miles to-day
when day's oppression is not eased by night.
So come my soul to bliss, as I speak true.

If it appear not plain and prove untrue,
that so my sad decrees may fly away,
kill me to-morrow: let me live to-night!
Thou livest; report me and my cause aright.
Why didst thou promise such a beauteous day?
If thou say so, withdraw, and prove it, too.

Let me have audience for a word or two:
this above all: to thine ownself be true.
Yet I confess that often ere this day,
in cases of defence, 'tis best to weigh,
to look into the blots and stains of right,
in high-born words the worth of many a knight.

The mountain or the sea, the day or night—
one side will mock another; the other, too.
O, let me, true in love, but truly write
without all ornament, itself and true,
for fear their colours should be washed away,
as are those dulcet sounds in break of day.

The nightingale, if she should sing by day,
and she died singing it: that song to-night,
which by and by black night doth take away;
if she pertain to life, let her speak, too!
They would not take her life—is this not true?
O, blame me not, if I no more can write!

Never durst poet touch a pen to write:
we are but warriors for the working-day.
If what I now pronounce you have found true:
when the sun sets, who doth not look for night?
Please you, deliberate a day or two,
let thy fair wisdom, not thy passion sway.

There is no other way: do me this right—
and it must follow, as the night the day,
write till your ink be dry. O, 'tis too true.

ALL THESE WORDS

after Richard Wilbur

      Agreed that all these words—
verb and adjective, noun and preposition—
    align premeditated on the page;
    each sound, each sememe willing to engage
    the silence of the surds;
                        that the metrician
        may be a dying breed,
        a dodo bird. Agreed

      that it is, in fact, a plan,
a scheme, a plot which, whether dastardly or not,
    attempts to order chaos via metre,
    just like the other wordsmiths (only neater)
    with words that rhyme and scan.
                 An afterthought:
        agreed the lines are drawn—
        it's owl versus swan.

      But let us part as friends,
Dear Reader, for the pure word's sake; for the design
    or lack thereof, and for the sake of love;
    for hawk and lark, for sparrow, stork and dove;
    for what transcends
                 the stanza, line,
        and for the hope that sings
        through words and feathered things.

A MOTHER'S KYRIELLE

For moments when they questioned me
and I replied indifferently,
or wished I'd practiced birth control,
       may God have mercy on my soul.

For little mouths washed out with soap,
for loss of patience, faith and hope,
for all the times I botched my role,
       may God have mercy on my soul.

For bad example, worse advice,
for thinking love would not suffice,
for every failure to console,
       may God have mercy on my soul.

And though it's true I've yelled and screamed,
the sad ranks of the unredeemed
can't count on me to shovel coal
       should God have mercy on my soul.

WHEN

For man also knoweth not his time. (Ecclesiastes)

the silver cord
the broken lamp
the overboard
the firedamp

the golden bowl
the unbeknown
the grassy knoll
the chicken bone

the shivered wheel
the shattered jar
the broken keel
the cattle car

the poor, the rich
the swift, the slack
the cur, the bitch
the heart attack

the weak, the strong
the sisters grim
the toll, the gong
the seraphim

remember Him

BOXING DAY PRAYER

We line up early, push and shove,
corral the cut-rate things we love;
forget the price You had to pay,
the cost incurred but yesterday.

And as we reach the checkout rows
with next year's tinsel, bells and bows,
forgive us that our vision fails
to see beyond the red tag sales.

RUSH HOUR SONONDILLA

I celebrate the great sardine
and count the ways I love it: dried,
in cans, smoked, salted, deep-fat fried,
filleted in soup and fish terrine.
I love its pre-cooked beauties, too—
its sleek and shiny silver skin,
its single tiny dorsal fin—
before it hits the barbecue.

Young herring, swimming in the sea,
awash in your Omega-3,
soon you shall pay a hefty price
and end up on a bed of rice.
For now, take heart in that you're free,
not packed inside this train, like me.

SHE

She is the one, the pride of Mr. Clean,
more finicky than Harriet and June
were in the fifties. Her discreet routine
won't find her drinking in the afternoon.
She is the one who, rosary in hand,
can pray in Latin, who reports each cent
she's earned or spent, may seem a trifle bland,
has no regrets and nothing to resent.

She is the one who takes things in her stride,
who metes out benefits of doubt, who sees
the glass half full, who is a bona fide
believer in the bright side. Sorry. She's
the one with wings who came out of the sky
and took up residence on Earth, not I.

IN RETROSPECT

for Hugo on our 40th wedding anniversary

Today I found that picture of us two;
the faded shot we'd taken in a booth
at Métro Laurier a week before
our baby's birth. In sepia tones suspended
in time, we smile our crazy love on cue—
a study in naiveté and youth.

Four decades later. Now we know the score.
With hopes and dreams come true (and some upended),
perhaps a formal portrait's overdue—
one that has us staring down the truth
with presbyopic eyes, a metaphor
for death. No, thanks. This old one's simply splendid—
a fitting witness to a man and wife
holding on to each other. For dear life.

PART V
A SMACK OF ALL NEIGHBOURING LANGUAGES

Five French Canadian (Québec) Poets

MY CHILDHOOD HOME

I visited our rustic home again.
The poplars tall as Gothic spires had grown;
the little fenced-in garden I had known
when I was young bloomed as it did back then.

A part of me had never left this site
where as a boy I sang without a care.
I passed the hearth, and stoked the embers there;
fond memories rekindled, warm and bright.

My awkward impudence seemed shameless, rude.
The children laughed at me; they could not know
their home was mine those many years ago.

I took my leave in a sad and sombre mood.
As I looked back once more, they shouted, "Oh,
why is that white-haired old man weeping so?"

*from the French "La maison paternelle" by Léon-Pamphile Le May (*Les gouttelettes, *1904)*

NIAGARA

How slowly the majestic river flows,
deceptive in its undulating roll;
for suddenly it loses all control,
collapsing to the thunderous depths below.

Behold the falls! No peaceful water hole
for errant birds that face its raging throes
then flee in fear the fiery scarf that bows
above the daunting chasm's misty bowl.

All trembles as this flood of liquid jade
transforms into a mountainous froth cascade
in frantic, fuming, fierce and booming song…

And yet, my God, this torrent you've set free,
that shatters rock, upends the grand oak tree,
in mercy spares the straw it whisks along.

from the French "Le Niagara" by Louis-Honoré Fréchette
*(*Les fleurs boréales; les oiseaux de neige, *1881)*

THE STARS

On sleepy summer evenings, when the blue
subsides to burnished gold or opaline
repose, a star appears in shy debut
to hang its torch above the quiet scene.

Then legions muster for the rendezvous
and take position. Soon a brilliant sheen
of diamonds turns the dusky vault into
the mantle of an oriental queen.

O Stars, perennials of outer space,
who cheer the silent night with lullabies,
who calm our fears and light each sombre place,

once you have risen in the glimmering skies
I am at peace, for I believe I trace
God's never-ending love within your eyes.

from the French "Les étoiles" by Louis Dantin
(Le coffret de Crusoé, 1932)

IT'S RAINING

This dismal autumn day the rain
is strophes. Poets, hold your hearts
like baskets out, despite your pain—
those scarlet wounds the world imparts!

Hold out your hearts to catch each drop;
collect the verses as they ring
with golden rhyme, before they stop.
Oh, let it rain on everything!

It rains in rhythm down the skies
in tender cadences of words
that chant the lilting lullabies,
like rushing wings of flitting birds.

For fellow poets, though we be
a woeful lot, the heavens bless
us with this proof of amity,
and pity our unhappiness.

So, you who hunt the volatile
idea, you who set it down
in perfect phrase, exquisite style,
like rubies in a burnished crown,

hold out your hearts: for poetry
is raining down in golden rhyme,
in incandescent prosody.
And may it rain! Rain all the time!

from the French "Il pleut" by Albert Lozeau
(L'âme solitaire, 1907)

THE PASSERBY

Last night a woman passed me in the park,
a veil of mourning shadowing her face.
Dispirited, she walked the sombre place
alone, her pride dissembled in the dark.

I could not help but guess as to the stark
adversity she dared not have me trace.
She sensed my scrutiny, stepped up her pace,
fled down an alleyway, beyond remark.

My youth is like this woeful passerby—
many shall cross my path before I die;
they shall observe me fade and fall and curl

like dry leaves in the whirlwind of the night;
while I, disconsolate, shall ever swirl
unloved, misunderstood, out of their sight.

from the French "La passante" by Émile Nelligan
 (Émile Nelligan et son oeuvre, *1903)*

Five Spanish American (Southern Cone) Women Poets

THE MYSTERIOUS STAR

I know not where it is, but it beckons me,
oh mysterious star of changeless destiny!...
Its hidden blaze and secret, unseen flame
in holy silent echo calls my name.

And if at times I leave the beaten track,
with an unknown force it always pulls me back:
chimera, phoenix, oriflamme and glory,
or love, beyond reach, strange and transitory...

I walk forever down an empty street
behind the fatal star that guides my feet
but never, never, never shows its light!

And yet its light calls out, its silence charms;
it summons me, while in the dark, my arms
in blind, despairing hope drag through the night.

*from the Spanish "La estrella misteriosa" by María Eugenia
Vaz Ferreira (*La isla de los cánticos, *1925)*

THE WONDERFUL BOAT

Build me a boat as lofty as a thought…
then name her *Star* or else *Obscurity*.
The whimsies of the wind and hand must not
command a craft as bold and fair as she!

She'll move to the pulsation of a heart
incarnadine with fierce vitality;
she'll make me strong as in the arms of God.
Trimmed to the wind her sails must always be!

I'm loading all my sorrow in my boat;
with no set course, a lotus flower, I'll float
along the vague horizon of the sea…

O Boat, my Soul Mate, what uncharted land,
what unexpected truths may lie at hand?…
This life, these dreams, shall be the death of me…

from the Spanish "La barca milagrosa" by Delmira Agustini
*(*Cantos de la mañana, *1910)*

THE SONNETS OF DEATH (I)

Men put you in an icy tomb, but I
will lower you to the humble, sunny earth.
They did not understand that, when I die,
we'll share one pillow and one dream in death.

I'll lay you gently in the sunlit ground,
as a mother puts her sleeping son to bed,
the soil soft upon your every wound,
a cradle for a child, though he be dead.

Then I will sprinkle rose dust with the loam,
and underneath the moon's blue-tinted glow,
your slight remains shall keep. In joyous tones

I'll sing my sweet revenge as I turn home,
because no other woman's hand shall claw
so deep to wrest from me your meagre bones!

*from the Spanish "Los sonetos de la muerte" by Gabriela
Mistral (1914)*

INHERITANCE

You told me: father never wept;
you said: grandfather would not wail;
men of my race have never cried,
they're made of steel.

And as you said these words, your tear
fell on my lips… such bitter gall
I've never tasted from another
cup so small.

This poor, weak woman drank, for I
to centuries of pain relate:
but oh, my soul cannot withstand
its crushing weight!

from the Spanish "Peso ancestral" by Alfonsina Storni
*(*Irremediablemente, *1919)*

REBEL

Charon: I'll be a scandal in your barque.
Those other souls may pray, lament or cry
beneath your evil patriarchal eye,
while timid spirits murmur in the dark.

Not I. I'll be the lark that flits and sings.
I'll flaunt my savage musk, and I will beam
my bright blue lantern on the bleak black stream,
sailing above the crossing on my wings.

You may not like it; and although you glare
at me with baleful eyes, I just don't care.
Charon, in your barque I'll be a scandal.

Then, when I'm cold and weak and fight no more,
your arms will drop me on the other shore—
vanquished—like the captive of a Vandal.

from the Spanish "Rebelde" by Juana de Ibarbourou
*(*Las lenguas de diamante, *1919)*

PART VI
GLAD &
SORRY
SEASONS

THE LOST VILLAGES: INUNDATION DAY

The water's rising...
They blew up the last cofferdam this morning,
so the water's rising, rising,
and our fields are disappearing forever.

Because they blew up the last cofferdam this morning,
nine villages and hamlets
and our fields are disappearing, forever
hushed by the St. Lawrence.

Nine villages and hamlets,
farms, forests and footprints
hushed by the St. Lawrence.
Six hundred homes and six thousand folk displaced.

Farms, forests and footprints
will lie under a wider, deeper Seaway;
six hundred homes and six thousand folk displaced
to the new towns of Ingleside and Long Sault.

Under the wider, deeper Seaway
are new currents and shoals,
new as Ingleside. But the Long Sault Rapids
no longer sing.

Currents and shoals are new,
but the old men who lived and worked along the river
no longer sing.
They are watching and waiting in silence from the hill.

The old men who lived and worked along the river
watch and wait in silence as flocks of shrieking birds
circle over the hill,
and the children stop their ears.

Flocks of shrieking birds
and the little animals of the fields are running for their lives,
children are stopping their ears,
and the women are weeping.

The little animals of the fields are running, for their lives
will never be the same,
and the women are weeping
over our lost villages.

Our lives will never be the same—
the water's rising, rising
over our lost villages.
Oh, how the water's rising!

UPHEAVALS

The February 27, 2010 magnitude 8.8 earthquake in Chile moved Earth's figure axis by about 3 inches, affecting the Earth's rotation, shortening its days, and moving the city of Concepción at least 10 feet to the West. (from NASA website)

The dire catastrophe—the flood, the quake,
the hurricane—is hailed as breaking news;
but unreported wrecks—the hearts that break
more quietly, those worlds of Waterloos,
those galaxies of grief, of x'd-off days—
outnumber each spectacular *KABOOM!*
that shocks and awes and tends to paraphrase
the terms of our unmentionable doom.

Our children, too, will one day come to know
that there are strings attached to happiness
and to the puppets in the puppet show;
a subtle shift in rapture, when they'll guess
at Something Out There, which in time devours
the careful crust of uneventful hours.

HEARTWOOD

For the woman with a blanket over her head, parked
in a wheelchair in the hallway of the Wesley Village Nursing Home.

When she was young she used to know
the Latin name for mistletoe;
loved both the bloom, the chestnut bur,
the grackle's caw, the cricket's chirr,
the sun, the storm, the afterglow.

And still the seasons come and go;
the *Pyrus* in her orchard grow
another ring, another spur.
When she was young

she tended them. Then came the snow.
Now, in a frail voice, tremolo,
she whispers "pear" as if it were
ineffable as petrichor,
as time tilts back to long ago
when she was young.

THE RED BEADS

Among the pipes and pulleys, sacks and seeds,
there is a necklace made of crimson beads.
Great care was taken that it catch the eye
of plain-clad *fernandinas* passing by
the Sunday market stalls and sundry shops
where needs and wants diverge. A woman stops.

She holds the necklace to her collar, asks
the price, then gently puts it down and masks
her disappointment with a repartee—
Demasiado lindo para mí.
Too nice. Yet, homeward-bound, she'll look again
and hope no one has bought it.
                                        Now and then,
a thing of beauty must be bargained for,
though all it graces is a dresser drawer.

RAGBAG

In remembrance of Charles Baudelaire

His is an art of foraging for rags,
for scrap and speck, for smithereen and shard,
for snippets gathered up in bales and bags
straining to hold what tidy lives discard.
He drags his pickings home, *capotes, mégots,*
an old *écu*, a button or a key;
then fashions sonnets and the odd rondeau,
master of a dubious alchemy.

So, blessed be the boy who banks, at best,
his smoldering fires of fancy with the fuel
of sensibility; and in his call
to be the city's ragman, may his quest
permit a vision that transcends the pool
of vomit, to the flower in the wall.

BEACH DOGS

In memory of Alfonsina Storni

A man parades his paunch, and you can bet
his wife, though dripping gold, will not get wet.
While brother reads *Clarín*, a bored boy pokes
a jellyfish. Grandma smirks and smokes.

They seem to sense that I'm not one of them;
I'm much too serious, too plain. *¡Ajém!*
I hear them warn each other as I rise
to shift my chair. They weigh my *gringa* thighs.

What's this I see? A scrawny mongrel winds
his way along the shore. At last he finds
a spot of shade. The worn-down, worn-out fella
drops down beneath the nearest beach umbrella.

Mine. My neighbours bray in disapproval,
insist upon the vagabond's removal;
then take a different tack and whisper, *Please…*
maybe he has the rabies or the fleas!

That well may be. For look—his skin is bruised
and scarred; he's been forgotten, shunned, abused.
I feed the dog some water and a crust
as the *porteños* gawk in dark disgust.

Before the Prefectura comes we fly,
he to the sands of Mansa Beach; while I,
cast off, adrift, unmoored from the décor,
will drown at sea and later wash ashore.

(Punta del Este, Uruguay, January 2009)

CRÍONNACHT

Though leaves are many, the root is one;
Through all the lying days of my youth
I swayed my leaves and flowers in the sun;
Now I may wither into the truth.

"The Coming of Wisdom with Time"—W.B. Yeats

I have done with blossoms.
I have done with boughs
overladen with sweetness.
I have done with unfoldings and ripenings.
I savour the sour and the bitter,
the rancid and the rotten.
Once and for all fandangles,
frills and fripperies are gone—
I have cut bedizenments to the bone.
Though leaves are many, the root is one,

reaching ever deeper to the core;
but in summertime it was the leaves
that spoke their bliss to me,
and I listened and I followed.
Bearings were relative—
a paradox, an azimuth—
while in my wanderings
I exalted crowns and canopies,
passing over the undergrowth
through all the lying days of my youth.

And lies they were,
with their false reflected colour:
a pitiful, leftover, extraneous colour,
the colour of camouflage,
the colour of envy, the colour of death;
not little white lies, but green.
Verde que te quiero verde… O hopeful green stuff…
All summer long, living indifferent
to the waxing and the waning of the moon,
I swayed my leaves and flowers in the sun.

Now all those swaying, swaggering leaves
have fallen to the ground.
They are being raked and bagged and dragged along.
They are being burnt in metal drums.
They are being swept up by the wind
hither and thither along a path
prepared by sickle and scythe,
seeking to strike an old man's knees.
Now there are bonfires on the heath.
Now I may wither into the truth.

WAITING

For the man in the Intensive Care Unit waiting room,
Hôpital Notre-Dame, Montréal, June 2012

Some nights I've seen
a slice of silver slink across this room
I now call home,
above my makeshift bed—a rickety chair
beside the snack machine.
Close by, the elevators whirr and beep.
I cannot, dare not, drift asleep,
let down my guard,
inviting shoulder taps, a whispered *Sir*,
or dreams of her
once-vivid eyes that stare & stare & stare,
dull, distant, hard.
Thus I will will her through another day.
Make crazy compromises. Pray.

EDWARD HOPPER'S *AUTOMAT*

One does not see the gleaming wall of glass,
its nickel slots and plates of apple pie,
the scores of harried customers who pass.
Reflected in the window's blackened eye,
two rows of matching ceiling fixtures light
a way to nowhere through the city night.

Inscrutable as an unsculptured stone,
between the brass-railed stairway and the door,
we see a woman sitting all alone,
a quiet presence in a stark décor.
Her posture mimics, spiritless and still,
the fresh fruit posing on the window sill.

A little radiator crouches near
the wall, and yet the woman wears a glove,
a knee-length, fur-trimmed coat, a hat. Career
girl? Actress? Maybe she's in love...
She's staring far beyond the coffee cup.
I wonder if some man has stood her up.

The empty wooden chair, the empty plate,
the downcast eyes beneath the cloche's brim,
suggest he was expected. Now it's late,
and any prospect of his coming's grim.
She weighs her options, as she slowly sips
and seems to pout with daubed vermilion lips.

Perhaps she can't find work, and soon must pack
her dreams and bags and board a Greyhound bound
for where she swore she never would go back.
Perhaps it's just her favourite stomping ground
where no one blinks at tables set for one;
where one can wallow in oblivion.

I want to tell her that I know. I know
she can survive whatever's brought her here;
that glad and sorry seasons come and go;
that there is nothing and no one to fear—
I've owned the loss, I've worn the coat and hat.
I am the woman in the automat.

NOTES

To a Minor Goddess: Achelois is a minor Greek moon goddess whose name, translated into English, means "she who washes away pain."

O: The Guaraní are the indigenous peoples of Paraguay.

Intervals: "Stacks" are used to solve problems involving nested structures; for example, to analyze an arithmetical expression containing subexpressions in parentheses, or to work out a route between two points when there are many different paths.

Haiku: Haru, natsu, aki, fuyu are the Japanese words for spring, summer, autumn and winter, respectively.

Breva: The breva (early fig) crop is the first fruit of the fig tree, developing in the spring on the previous year's shoot growth.

Winterbourne: A winterbourne is a stream, typically on chalk or limestone, which flows only after wet weather, especially in winter.

Superbia: *Tant pis!* in English means *Too bad!*

Acedia: DINK is the acronym for Dual Income No Kids.

The Bard is a cento/sestina or a sestina/cento, all lines taken verbatim from the works of William Shakespeare.

Rush Hour Sonondilla: The sonondilla, also known as the Redondilla Sonnet, the Napoleonic Sonnet, the Corsican Sonnet, and the Sardinian Sonnet (or simply, "the Sardine"), is a cross between a Petrarchan sonnet and the redondilla. The Sardine is purely syllabic verse as is the redondilla. Each line has eight syllables. It can be iambic, trochaic, spondaic, phyrric, amphibrachic, pæonic, pharoanic, or any other accents or lack of accentual metre. The rhyme scheme is either abbacddceeffee or abbaabbaccddcc.

She: Harriet and June refer to Harriet Nelson (of *The Adventures of Ozzie and Harriet)* and June Cleaver (of *Leave It to Beaver)*, idealized suburban housewives of two mid-20th century American sitcoms.

The Lost Villages: Inundation Day: By government decree, the Ontario, Canada villages of Mille Roches, Moulinette, Wales, Dickinson's Landing, Farran's Point and Aultsville; the hamlets of Maple Grove, Santa Cruz and Woodlands; and the farming community of Sheik's Island were inundated on July 1, 1958 for the sake of the St. Lawrence Seaway and an international hydroelectric project. These communities are known collectively as "The Lost Villages."

Heartwood: The heartwood of a tree is the central core hardwood around which the annual concentric rings grow. A tree can thrive with its heart completely decayed. Petrichor is defined as the pleasant scent of rain on dry earth.

The Red Beads: a *fernandina* is a woman of San Fernando de Maldonado, a small working-class city adjoining the luxury resort of Punta del Este, Uruguay.

Ragbag: *capotes, mégots,* and *écu* translated into English are, respectively, condoms, cigarette butts, and an old French coin bearing the figure of a shield.

Beach Dogs: *Clarín* is a daily newspaper published in Buenos Aires, Argentina. *Porteños* are residents of Buenos Aires, as opposed to other regions of Argentina. Porteños are often portrayed as snobbish, arrogant and self-centred. Alfonsina Storni, Swiss-born Argentine poet, committed suicide by drowning herself at Mar del Plata, Argentina, in 1938.

Críonnacht: The word críonnacht is Gaelic for wisdom. The poem is a glosa.

ACKNOWLEDGMENTS

These poems, often in significantly different versions, have previously appeared, or are forthcoming, in the following journals and magazines:

14 by 14, Able Muse Journal, Angle Poetry Journal, Antiphon, Blue Unicorn, The Centrifugal Eye, The Chimaera, First Things, The Flea, Fox Chase Review, The HyperTexts, Iambs and Trochees, Innisfree Poetry Journal, Lost Villages Newsletter, Lucid Rhythms, The Lyric, Measure, Mezzo Cammin, Orbis, Per Contra, Quadrant, The Raintown Review, String Poet, Sunday @ Six Magazine, Texas Poetry Journal, Umbrella.

The author wishes to thank the editors, as well as fellow members of the Greenwood Poets and Eratosphere, for their generosity and support.

CATHERINE CHANDLER was born in New York City, raised in Wilkes-Barre, Pennsylvania and has lived and worked in Canada since 1972. She completed her postgraduate studies at McGill University, where she taught in the Department of Translation Studies for many years and acted as the University's International Affairs Officer. She also taught Spanish at Concordia University.

Winner of the Howard Nemerov Sonnet Award, The Lyric Quarterly Prize, and six-time Pushcart Prize nominee, Catherine's poetry, essays and literary translations from French and Spanish have appeared in numerous journals and anthologies in the United States, the United Kingdom, Canada and Australia. She is the author of *For No Good Reason* and *All or Nothing,* and is co-editor of *Passages: A Collection of Poems by the Greenwood Poets* (The Greenwood Centre for Living History, 2010). Her first full-length collection of poetry, *Lines of Flight,* published by Able Muse Press in April 2011, was shortlisted for the 2013 Poets' Prize, and a collection of sonnets, *This Sweet Order,* was published by White Violet Press in 2012.

Catherine currently lives in Saint-Lazare, Québec.